BL 5.5
pt. 1.0

Lill's Book

1,00
8-1
D

# Lions

## NATURE'S PREDATORS

Kris Hirschmann

KidHaven Press, an imprint of Gale Group, Inc.
P.O. Box 289009, San Diego, CA 92198-9009

**Library of Congress Cataloging-in-Publication Data**

Hirschmann, Kris, 1967–
    Lions / by Kris Hirschmann.
      p. cm. — (Nature's Predators)
    Includes bibliographical references (p.   )
    ISBN 0-7377-0540-X (hardback : alk. paper)
    1. Lions—Juvenile literature. [1. Lions.] I. Title. II. Nature's
    Predators (San Diego, Calif.)
    QL737.C23 H57 2002
    599.757—dc21

    00-012809

**Picture Credits**
Cover Photo: © Philip Berry/Anthony Banister Photo Library/Photo Researchers
© Paul Almasy/Corbis, 39
© Yann Arthus-Bertrand/Corbis, 19, 21
© W. Perry Conway/Corbis, 41
© Alissa Crandall/Corbis, 37
© Digital Stock, 27
© John Farmar/Ecoscene/Corbis, 11, 23
© Robert W. Hernandez/Photo Researchers, 18
© Stephen J. Krasemann/Photo Researchers, 13
© Joe McDonald/Corbis, 16, 35
© Mary Ann McDonald/Corbis, 4
© Amos Nachoum/Corbis, 29
© Stan Osolinski, 1993/FPG International, 6
© Planet Earth Pictures, 1998/FPG International, 33
© Mitch Reardon/Photo Researchers, 26
© Lynda Richardson/Corbis, 9
Martha E. Schierholz, 7, 8, 14, 30
© Sandro Vannini/Corbi, 40

# Contents

# Chapter 1

## Killers in Cat Disguise

L ions look a lot like giant house cats. This makes sense, because lions and cats are relatives. Lions are sometimes even called "big cats." Their magnificent looks and muscular bodies have given them another nickname, too: the "King of Beasts." It is a good nickname. These proud creatures rule the animal world wherever they make their home.

But a lion's sweet, catlike looks and beautiful body hide its true nature. Lions are not friendly, and they are not pets. They are dangerous predators, ready and able to kill on a moment's notice.

Most of the time, lions are lazy. During the hot daylight hours, they can usually be found resting in the shade of a scrubby tree.

During the day, lions take it easy. Once night falls they become active.

---

But everything changes when dusk arrives. The lions stretch, becoming alert and restless. The lionesses pace back and forth. The adult males roar loudly and shake their thick, dark manes. They seem to be announcing that they are awake and hungry. Soon the lions will hunt, and few creatures are safe when hungry lions roam.

## What's for Dinner?

Lions are carnivores. This means that they eat other animals. They eat a *lot* of other animals. Lions are usually hungry, and they are always on the lookout for the next meal.

The "next meal" depends on where a lion lives and what kind of prey lives in the area. A small number of lions live in India's Gir Forest. They are called Asiatic lions, and they are considered highly endangered. There are only about three hundred Asiatic lions left in the world. These lions eat mostly deer, which are very common in the Gir. They also eat domestic cattle whenever they can break into the farms that surround their territory.

Africa is where most of the world's lions live. No one is sure exactly how large the African lion population is. But researchers guess that the number is somewhere between thirty thousand and a hundred thousand animals.

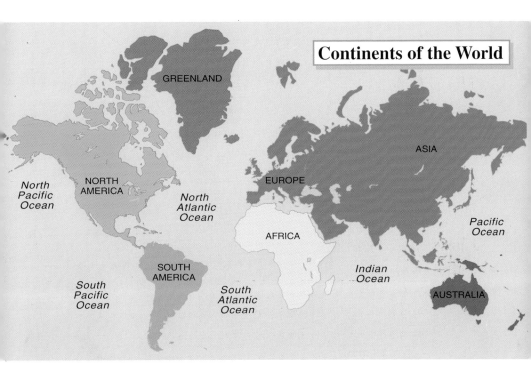

Continents of the World

African lions can be found in many different types of terrain. Some live in woodland areas. Others make their homes on the grassy African plains. Still others scratch out a living in the hot, dry Kalahari Desert.

The African lion's diet changes from region to region and season to season. Although these lions

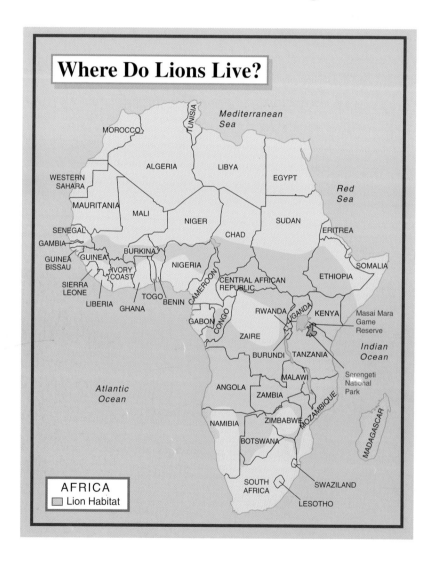

**Where Do Lions Live?**

MOROCCO
TUNISIA
Mediterranean Sea
ALGERIA
LIBYA
WESTERN SAHARA
EGYPT
Red Sea
MAURITANIA
MALI
NIGER
SENEGAL
SUDAN
GAMBIA
CHAD
ERITREA
GUINEA BISSAU
GUINEA
BURKINA
NIGERIA
SOMALIA
SIERRA LEONE
IVORY COAST
CAMEROON
CENTRAL AFRICAN REPUBLIC
ETHIOPIA
LIBERIA
TOGO
BENIN
GHANA
GABON
CONGO
RWANDA
UGANDA
KENYA
Masai Mara Game Reserve
ZAIRE
Indian Ocean
BURUNDI
TANZANIA
Atlantic Ocean
MALAWI
Serengeti National Park
ANGOLA
ZAMBIA
MOZAMBIQUE
NAMIBIA
ZIMBABWE
MADAGASCAR
BOTSWANA
SOUTH AFRICA
SWAZILAND
LESOTHO

AFRICA
☐ Lion Habitat

seem to like zebras, gazelles, wildebeests, buffalo, and warthogs the best, they do not always get a choice. During the rainy season, when grass grows tall on the plains, herds of grazing animals are easy to find. Lions can afford to be picky and hunt only their favorite prey. But during the dry season, lions must hide around water holes and wait for thirsty animals to show up. In times like these, lions will take whatever prey comes along.

## Not Too Big, Not Too Small

Lions choose prey mostly because of size, not taste. They prefer animals that are large enough to make

Lions are smart enough not to attack larger and stronger animals such as elephants.

a good meal, but small enough to catch without too much trouble or danger.

They ignore very large creatures such as adult elephants, hippopotamuses, rhinoceroses, and giraffes. These animals are big enough and strong enough to defend themselves from the lion's attack. They can hurt or even kill a lion. But a baby hippo or elephant is fair game. And every once in a while, lions do catch a large animal if it is very sick or old. A pride of lions can feast for days on the dead body, or carcass, of one of these big animals.

Small animals are usually ignored, too. Little creatures such as birds, turtles, and fish are not much of a meal for a full-grown lion. But a really hungry lion will eat them if it cannot find anything bigger. It will even lick up insects if no other food is available.

Lions are not always hungry, and they are not always in the mood to hunt. Other animals seem to know this and will sometimes graze near sleepy lions. But they never forget that any lion, even a resting one, can be deadly.

## Armed and Dangerous

Why are lions so dangerous? It is because they have a great many tools that help them to chase and catch their prey.

The lion's sharp teeth and claws are its most powerful weapons. A lion has thirty teeth. Four of these teeth are long, pointed fangs called canines. The canines can easily break the skin of the lion's

Armed with sharp teeth and claws, lions are extremely dangerous.

prey. Four sharp claws on each foot can also grab and tear. The lion pulls these curved claws back into special pockets in its paws when they are not being used. This keeps them razor sharp and ready to slash at all times.

A lion uses its teeth and claws to hold on to prey. With these weapons sunk deep into an animal's flesh, a lion is almost impossible to shake off.

## Seeing, Hearing, Smelling

Before the lion can catch its prey, though, it must find it. That is where the lion's excellent eyesight, hearing, and sense of smell come in handy.

Lions have the largest eyes of any carnivore. They see very well with these big eyes. In fact, they can probably see five to six times better than humans. During daylight hours, lions may spot prey far across the plains. They may also see vultures circling high in the blue sky. The birds would be tiny, meaningless specks to a person—but to a lion, they point to a meal. Vultures are scavengers that feed on dead animals. When they spot a sick or hurt animal, they circle patiently, waiting for the animal to die. For this reason, a vulture in the air means food on the ground below. Without good eyes, lions might miss this important clue.

Lions can see even better in the dark than in bright conditions. Their eyes are built to capture as much light as possible. As a result, they can see well even on the blackest night. Most daytime animals have very poor night vision. This makes them easy pickings for lions during the dark night hours. For this reason, lions usually hunt at night. They are also active just after dusk and just before dawn.

Although lions usually find their prey by sight, hearing also helps. A lion may hear an animal walking through dry, rustling grass or splashing through a creek. It may also hear the cries of a hurt animal. When lions hear sounds like these, they usually rush to investigate. Many times they find a meal.

Lions may even use their sense of smell to find prey. Scientists have seen lions tracking prey by raising their heads and sniffing the air. But this is not common. Lions probably use smell as a last resort.

## Killing Machines

All these tools make lions skilled killing machines. Yet they sometimes go days without catching food. The reason lies in the one big advantage some other

---

Lions have four claws on each foot, which they use to grab and hang on to prey.

## How Fast Do Lions Run?

Human

Lion

Cat

Zebra

Cheetah

| 20 | 28 30 | 35 | 40+ | 60 | 70 | 80 |

**Miles Per Hour**

animals have over lions. Most animals that lions hunt can run much faster than the lions. Lions can go thirty-five miles per hour for a short burst, but zebras, gazelles, and other prey may reach speeds up to fifty miles per hour. If a lion does not get a good head start, its prey will just outrun it.

Lions make up for this disadvantage by being smart, skillful, and strong. These qualities make them excellent hunters.

# Chapter 2

# On the Hunt

When night approaches, lions become alert. It is time to hunt.

Wild lions live and hunt together in groups called prides. A pride consists of two or more adult males, two or more lionesses, and many cubs under two years of age. All of the lionesses in a pride are usually related to one another. The adult males may also be related to one another, but not to the lionesses.

A big pride can contain as many as forty members. But that is unusually large. A typical pride contains around twenty lions.

Each pride of lions has its own hunting territory. The size of the territory depends on the

Even while this pride of lions rests in the grass, each member watches the plain for dinner.

quality of the hunting. In a good area with lots of prey, a pride's territory may be as small as ten square miles. But lions must travel farther to find food in less populated areas. In the Kalahari Desert, for example, a pride's territory may be as large as 150 square miles.

The pride wanders through its territory for several hours each night, usually covering four to five miles between dusk and dawn. Males, females, and cubs walk together. They travel slowly, without any set destination. They will walk until they are tired, or until they find food—whichever comes first.

Although the whole pride goes along on the nightly hunt, it is the females who will do most of the work. Males are good hunters and can kill if necessary, but they usually hang back and let the lionesses bring down the prey. This might be a simple matter of disguise. Females are smaller than males, and they do not have big, dark, furry manes that could be spotted by prey. These qualities probably make it easier for lionesses to sneak up on other animals.

## The Stalk

Lions have many hunting methods. On the plains, the method they choose depends mostly on the size of the prey.

Many animals are small enough to be caught and killed by a single lion. When one of these animals is spotted, a lion goes into a crouch and begins creeping toward the prey. It advances very slowly, carefully moving one paw at a time and making as little noise as possible. This advance is called the stalk.

During the stalk, the lion does everything it can to avoid being seen. It holds its body close to the ground. Its tawny fur blends into the brown grass of the plains, making it very hard to spot. And it keeps its tail tucked down so the black tuft at the tip will not give it away.

The lion keeps its eyes glued to the prey as it moves forward. If the animal shows the slightest sign of nervousness, the lion freezes. It stands as still as a statue until the prey relaxes. As soon as it does, the lion resumes the stalk.

This lion (bottom, center) blends with the grasses as it stalks the springbok and zebras.

The lion creeps forward until it gets within at least a hundred feet of its prey. Then its muscles tense. It gathers its strength and springs out of its hiding place. It rushes toward the prey with all its might. If the lion is lucky, its effort will pay off. It will outrun the prey and earn a meal.

## Group Hunting

About half of all hunting is done by single lions. The other half is done by groups of lions. Lions are the only cats that hunt in groups, and they are very good at it.

Some animals are too large to be killed by a single lion. When big prey is spotted, several lions will approach in a long line. They spread out as they get closer. The lions at the ends of the line walk faster, getting ahead of the others. Before long, the lions are arranged in a horseshoe shape around the prey. This is called encircling.

When all the lions are in place, one or two jump out, startling the prey. The frightened animal runs away—right into the jaws of the hidden hunters. Several lions then work together to bring the prey down.

Lions also work in groups when they hunt herds of smaller animals, such as gazelles. They may use their encircling trick. They have a simpler

Lionesses bring down a wildebeest. Lions are the only cats that hunt in groups.

strategy, though, that works just as well. Several lions approach the gazelles at the same time. They do not act especially threatening. They do not even try to make the herd move in any particular direction. But the gazelles know that lions mean danger. Just seeing them is enough to make the animals panic. They start running in all directions as they try to escape. With a little luck, a few terrified gazelles will run straight toward a hungry lion.

## The Ambush

Lions do not always chase their prey. Sometimes they hide and let their prey come to them. This hunting technique is called the ambush.

Water holes are favorite ambush spots. A lion settles into the long grass that surrounds the water hole. Then it waits for food to show up. When the time is right, the lion leaps from its hiding place and grabs the prey.

Unfortunately for the lion, other animals know that water holes are dangerous. They are very careful when they approach, and they keep a sharp lookout while they drink. If the lion moves, it may be seen. Yet it must be very near its prey before it can attack. So the lion sits perfectly still, waiting for an animal to wander too close. A lion may hide for hours before the right opportunity comes along.

## Catching and Killing

Lions do not catch every animal they hunt. In fact, they fail more often than they succeed. It is very common for a lion to rush at an animal, chase it for several hundred feet, and then abandon the chase as the quick-moving prey gets farther and farther away.

But of course, lions *do* catch up to their speedy prey from time to time. When they do, the prey has no chance against the lion's powerful body, claws, and teeth.

———

A lioness sinks her claws into the rump of a wildebeest as her pride looks on.

The chase begins when a lion explodes out of its hiding place in a cloud of dust. It rushes at its prey, teeth bared. The startled prey turns to run. It may escape if it gets a good head start. But if the lion is very close, the prey will not have enough time to build up any speed.

When the lion catches up to the fleeing animal, it leaps forward and upward with one mighty push of its powerful hind legs. The lion extends its sharp claws out of their sheaths as it leaps. It lands hard and sinks these claws into the rump of its prey, easily slashing through skin and flesh. The lion digs in deep and holds on tight.

The sheer impact is often enough to knock the prey off its feet. If the animal manages to stay upright, the lion jerks it sideways and makes it lose its balance. One way or the other, the prey soon falls to the ground.

Once the prey is down, the lion yanks backward on the animal's rump, pulling it closer. The lion then leaps onto the prey's body or up toward its head.

The lion kills small animals, such as birds, rodents, and some types of gazelles, with a hard bite to the back of the neck. This bite snaps the animal's spine and kills it instantly. But most of the lion's prey are too large to be killed this way. Animals such as wildebeests and zebras have big, thick necks that are not so easy to snap. To kill large prey, the lion locks its strong jaws around the prey's throat and clamps it tight. Then it settles down to

Lions kill with a bite to the neck.

wait. The lion is not trying to bite through the throat. It is using the power of its jaws to close the prey's air passage. The lion will hold its position until the prey is dead. This process may take ten minutes or even more, but the lion is patient. It sits calmly, biting hard, waiting for its prey to suffocate.

When the prey finally stops struggling, the lion releases its grip. It is time to eat.

# Chapter 3

# Dinnertime

During the hunt, the rest of the pride sits at a safe distance, watching. They look relaxed. But their eyes betray their interest. The lions gaze toward the action, following every move the hunters make. If the hunt is successful, there will be food. If not, the pride will go hungry.

The instant the prey goes down, all the lions rush to the kill site. They try to grab as much food as possible. They do not care who made the kill, and they do not care whether the other members of the pride get to eat. Each lion cares only about filling its own belly.

Pride members get along well most of the time. But everything is different when a meal is on the table. The lions are ready to fight for their share of the kill—and these fights can be vicious. Lions will bite and claw one another to get food. They may even give each other serious wounds during these fights.

## The Lion's Share

The biggest, strongest lions are able to take food away from the others. Males are usually the biggest lions in the pride. For this reason, the males normally eat first, and they usually get the largest portions (the "lion's share"). The females grab whatever the males have not claimed. If the kill is small, many lions will not get any food at all.

Most animals make sure their babies are fed. Lions, however, show no concern for their cubs at mealtime. The cubs have to fight for their food just like everyone else. But the cubs are much too small to compete with the grown lions. They must wait until all the adults are satisfied before they can eat. During times when food is scarce, cubs often starve to death.

Sometimes lions kill an animal that is large enough to feed the whole pride. When this happens, all the lions settle down around the carcass in a tight ring. Each lion eats from the part of the animal directly in front of it.

The lions gobble down the food as quickly as they can. And even though there is plenty to go around, the lions guard their portions jealously.

Even though lions live and hunt together, they will often fight over food.

While they eat, they keep a careful eye on the lions to either side. They snarl at their neighbors in between bites, warning them to stay away. Any lion that gets too close may earn a painful scratch.

## Hiding the Kill

Sometimes a lion manages to make a kill without being seen by the rest of the pride. This is good luck for the hunter. If the lion can keep its kill a secret, it gets a nice big meal that it does not have to share with the others.

The hunter knows, though, that it will be forced to give up part of its meal if the other lions find it. So instead of starting to eat right away, the lion may try to hide its kill. It is not unusual for lions to drag carcasses into bushes or tall grass, hoping to hide them from the rest of the pride.

Lions sometimes even try to fool the pride into thinking that a hunt was unsuccessful. A hunter that has just made a kill may sit casually near the fallen prey. It does not eat. It just looks around calmly. The other lions watch with interest at first. But they lose interest when they do not see the hunter eating. They think that no kill was made, and they soon wander

A male lion tries to keep his kill to himself by dragging it away and hiding it.

away. The minute they are gone, the hunter begins to feast.

## Nothing Is Wasted

To a predator, every scrap of food is precious. Stalking, chasing, and killing prey burns a lot of energy. And every bit of that energy must come from the muscles, organs, bones, blood, and skin of prey. So lions eat as many parts of a carcass as they possibly can. Almost nothing is wasted.

Lions start by eating the internal organs—the heart, liver, kidneys, and other viscera. Undigested food inside the stomach and intestines is not usually eaten. And lions do not seem to like the lungs as much as the other organs. Every now and then, they leave them lying uneaten. But all the other organs are tasty treats. They are gobbled up within minutes.

To reach these organs, lions sink their sharp teeth into the skin of the carcass, then pull hard to open holes in the animal's side. All the work is done by the mouth and teeth. Lions barely use their paws when they eat.

By the time the internal organs are gone, the ground is red with blood. So are the lions' muzzles. But the hungry predators are just getting started.

The lions next begin to eat the animal's muscles. They use their long canine teeth to pull huge chunks of muscle meat off the carcass. Lions have no teeth for chewing, so they swallow these

Lions will let no part of a prey go to waste. They will eat every part of this buffalo except the teeth.

chunks whole. They eat as quickly as they can. The faster they eat, the more food they will get.

When most of the meat is gone, the lions turn their attention to the bones. Now, finally, they begin to use their paws. They hold the bones steady between their powerful legs and paws, then use their rough tongues to lick every last scrap of meat off each bone. But even that is not enough. After the bones are scraped clean, the lions crunch the polished bones to pieces to get at the rich, meaty marrow inside.

The meal is finally over when the last bone has been chewed to splinters. The lions have eaten everything but the prey's horns, teeth, and a few shards of bone. From start to finish, it probably took less than thirty minutes for the lions to consume the carcass.

If the kill is large, everyone will get enough to eat. The pride will rest after the meal, enjoying their full stomachs. But if the kill is not big enough to feed everyone, the lions will move on after their meal. The hunt will continue as long as the lions are hungry.

## Big Eaters

Lions have big bodies. Not including the tail, a big male lion may be more than nine feet long and may weigh up to 550 pounds. Lionesses are a little smaller, but not much. These big bodies need a lot of fuel. So it is no surprise that lions

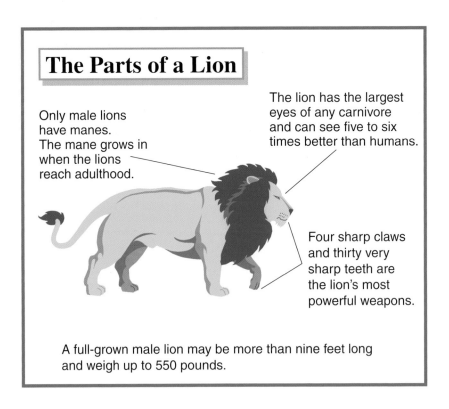

### The Parts of a Lion

Only male lions have manes. The mane grows in when the lions reach adulthood.

The lion has the largest eyes of any carnivore and can see five to six times better than humans.

Four sharp claws and thirty very sharp teeth are the lion's most powerful weapons.

A full-grown male lion may be more than nine feet long and weigh up to 550 pounds.

are big eaters. A large male lion needs as much as fifteen pounds of food per day.

A lion that has gone without food for several days does its best to make up for lost time. It is very common for a lion to eat forty-five pounds of food in one meal. And a really hungry lion may eat even more—up to seventy-five pounds of food at a single sitting. It takes the lion nearly five hours to eat such a gigantic meal. When a lion eats this much food, its stomach bulges out like an inflated balloon. The bloated predator must rest for a long time to digest its enormous dinner.

If the lions are very lucky, a kill may be too large for the pride to finish in one meal. When this happens, the lions will hang around until every scrap of meat is consumed. This may take days. During this time, the carcass sits in the hot sun. It starts to rot and smell bad. But the lions do not seem to mind. They are not picky about the freshness of their food. They will snack on the stinky carcass until it disappears.

# Chapter 4

# When Predator Becomes Prey

The strongest predators in an area are said to be at the top of the food chain. This means that they eat many other animals, but nothing eats them.

Lions are at the top of their food chain. They are not the only predators on the African plains, but they are the largest and the most powerful. Their size and their strength keep them safe. Hyenas, leopards, jackals, and other smaller predators will not attack a full-grown lion. And big animals that *could* harm a lion, such as elephants and rhinoceroses, are not killers by nature. They prefer to leave the lions alone.

So adult lions have fewer worries than most other animals. They still have to find food, but they are not likely to *become* food.

## Cubs in Danger

Lion cubs, however, are a different story. They are too small and too weak to protect themselves. Any cub that wanders away from the safety of the pride is in great danger. If it runs into another predator, it will be killed and eaten. And it may be trampled to death if it gets in the way of the hunt.

To protect her cubs, a lioness will sneak away from her pride to give birth and will return about six weeks later, when the cubs are strong enough to follow her.

The first threat a lion cub faces, though, does not come from other predators. It comes from the members of its own pride. Adult males often kill very young cubs.

To prevent this from happening, a lioness sneaks away from the pride when she is ready to have her babies. She gives birth in a secret lair. Her litter usually contains two to five small, blind, and completely helpless cubs. But the newborns grow quickly. By the time they are six weeks old, the cubs are strong enough to follow their mother around. The lioness returns to the pride, bringing her cubs with her. They are big enough now to be safe from the other members of the pride.

## Nomadic Lions

But the cubs are still in danger. Although they will not be harmed by members of their own pride, they are often killed by wandering, or *nomadic,* lions.

Lions do not become nomadic by choice. It happens because of the way lion society works. When young male lions are about two years old, the older males force them to leave the pride. The young males become wanderers. They live and hunt on their own. But as they get older, the nomadic lions grow bigger and stronger. After a while, they are powerful enough to try to take over another pride. They fight with the males of the pride, trying to kill them or at least drive them away.

Lion cubs face many threats and only the healthiest and strongest survive.

If the nomads succeed, they become the new leaders of the pride. Right away, they kill all the cubs. They do not want to waste their time and energy raising another male's offspring. They want to have the females of the pride to themselves, and they want to produce cubs of their own.

Nomadic lions are a big threat to cubs, but not the only one. Other predators such as leopards and hyenas will kill and eat lion cubs if they find them wandering away from the pride. Starvation is also a problem. About half of all lion cubs die because they do not get enough food.

It is sad that so many cubs die, but it is good for the lion population in the long run. Only the healthiest, strongest cubs survive, leading to healthy, strong adult lions in the future.

## The Human Threat

Even the strongest lion is no match for a human with a gun, however.

In the late 1800s, lion hunting became a popular sport. A hunter did not consider his trophy case to be complete unless it held the stuffed head of a lion. More and more people traveled to Africa from all over the world to shoot these magnificent creatures. And as the years passed, the lion population plunged.

Today people are not allowed to shoot lions for sport. Africa is now the home of many huge national parks where animals roam freely, safe from the hunter's gun. People still flock to these parks.

Tourists snap pictures of a male and female lion at Masai Mara Game Reserve in Kenya, Africa.

But instead of guns, they bring cameras. They also bring tourism dollars. The money they spend helps to keep the parks, and the animals that live there, alive.

The Serengeti National Park, the Masai Mara Game Reserve, and other protected animal havens have helped the lion population to bounce back and even thrive. African lions are no longer considered endangered.

But not all lions live in the parks. Those outside the boundaries of the protected areas are in constant danger from man. And even lions that live inside the national parks are not completely safe. As the human population of Africa increases, farms are springing up along the edges of the parks. Hungry lions sometimes go after the livestock on these farms. When they do, they are often killed by angry farmers. The killing of such "nuisance lions" is permitted by the governments of most African countries.

Farms also bring illness. Lions can easily catch some sicknesses that are carried by livestock and other farm animals. Rabies is one deadly, incurable disease that has affected the lion population. Another is canine distemper. Since 1994, this disease has killed as much as one-third of the lion population in some parts of Africa.

## Conservation Efforts

More and more farms mean less and less room for lions and other wild animals. Although African lions are not endangered, their territories are being squeezed. Researchers are afraid that the lion population will begin to shrink quickly if this trend continues.

The settlement of once-empty regions is not the only problem lions face. The national parks in some areas are in danger of shrinking or disappearing altogether. In some African countries, the human population is growing quickly, and hunger is a serious problem. People in these countries are putting a lot of pressure on their governments to turn parkland back into much-needed farmland. In other countries, people just ignore the park

Conservationists are trying to protect lions from farmers who see them as a threat to their livestock.

boundaries and build farms wherever they want. If the country is very poor, its government sometimes cannot afford to enforce its conservation laws.

Conservation groups in Africa are working hard to prevent the national parks from shrinking or disappearing. All wild animals, not just lions, need space to roam. Without it, many will die. So keeping the parks intact is an important step.

Conservationists are also trying to convince farmers to live peacefully alongside lions. One way they are doing this is by setting up programs that let

Conservation efforts include educating the public about lions while encouraging the animals to breed in zoos like this one in London.

farmers make money from the presence of lions. For instance, farmers may receive some of the tourism dollars that visitors spend when they come to Africa on safari. If the lions die, the tourists will not come anymore and the farmers will not be paid. Under this circumstance, farmers usually decide that it is better to put up with the lions than to kill them.

In Asia, the home of the endangered Asiatic lion, conservation efforts are much stronger. A special area called the **Gir Forest and Sanctuary** has been set aside as a home for these lions. The sanctuary is carefully monitored. No hunting of the Gir lions is permitted for any reason.

Zoos around the world also help by running captive breeding programs. In these programs, the zoos' Asiatic lions are encouraged to breed and raise families. These programs ensure that the Asiatic lion will never become extinct, even if the natural population is wiped out.

## Learning to Live Together

Researchers are at the heart of the conservation effort. These men and women spend long, hot,

Researchers place radio collars on lions in order to track their movements and learn more about them.

and sometimes dangerous hours in the field. They study lions in their natural habitat. They may even catch lions and fit them with radio collars. These special collars send out a signal that tells the researchers exactly where the lions are at all times. By tracking lions, researchers hope to learn more about their lives and habits.

Each year researchers discover new facts about lions. And this important work teaches others how to help lions survive—and thrive. With care and continued work, it may be possible to preserve these predators' traditional way of life long into the future.

# Glossary

**ambush:** A hunting technique that involves hiding and waiting for prey to approach.

**canines:** The four long, sharp fangs at the front of a lion's mouth.

**carcass:** A dead body.

**carnivore:** Any animal that eats other animals.

**conservation:** The planned protection of a natural resource. Natural resources take many forms, including places, materials, and animals.

**conservationist:** A person who works to support conservation efforts.

**cub:** A young lion.

**encircling:** A group hunting technique in which many lions spread out around prey.

**endangered:** In danger of becoming extinct.

**extinct:** A species becomes extinct when its last member dies. Conservationists hope to prevent this from happening.

**food chain:** The process that transfers energy to larger and larger animals. For example, grass takes energy from sunlight; gazelles eat the grass; lions eat the gazelles.

**lioness:** An adult female lion.

**nomadic lion:** Any lion that is not a member of a pride.

**predator:** Any animal that survives by killing and eating other animals.

**pride:** A family group of lions.

**scavenger:** Any animal that does not kill for food, but does find and eat animals that are already dead.

**stalk:** A lion's slow, stealthy approach of prey.

**territory:** The land area that a pride of lions will defend from other lions.

**viscera:** Internal organs.

# For Further Exploration

## Books

Amanda Harman, *Endangered! Lions*. New York: Benchmark Books, 1997.
> This book provides a good general look at lions and is filled with colorful pictures.

Cynthia Overback, *Lions: A Lerner Natural Science Book*. Minneapolis: Lerner Publications, 1981.
> This well-written book earned an award from the New York Academy of Sciences.

## Websites

**The Asiatic Lion Information Centre**
www.asiatic-lion.org.
> A central resource for information about one of India's most endangered big cats and the conservation efforts in progress to try to save it. There is also a good picture gallery.

**Big Cats Online**
http://dialspace.dial.pipex.com/agarman/main_ie.htm.
 This website provides good general information on all
 thirty-six species of wild cats.

**Lion Research Center**
www.lionresearch.org.
 The Lion Research Center provides general information about African and Asiatic lions. It also lists information on conservation efforts.

**Lion Videos**
www.safaricamlive.com/Encyclopedia/Mammals/
Lion/lion_movies.htm.
 More than fifty video clips to download. See and hear
 lions hunting, eating, playing, and more.

**World Wildlife Federation Global Network**
www.panda.org.
 The WWF is one of the biggest conservation organiza-
 tions in the world. This site contains information
 about the organization's efforts.

# Index